Falling in Love With Jesus

Falling in Love With Jesus

Rev. Dr. David Hartwell, Jr.

Companion Press
P.O. Box 310
Shippensburg, PA 17257-0310
Internet: http://www.reapernet.com

"Good Stewards of the
Manifold Grace of God"

ISBN 1-56043-580-1

For Worldwide Distribution
Printed in the U.S.A.

Dedication

To God, the Father of my Lord Christ Jesus who died that He could live in me.

To my wife Hattie M. Hartwell who never stops loving me and supporting me during the long hours I spend apart from her while in prayer and research in the Bible. I want to thank her. She is also a preacher and teacher of the gospel. My darling wife, Rev. Hattie M. Hartwell, I love you.

Rev. Dr. David Hartwell, Jr.

Contents

The Word Became Flesh:

In the beginning was the Word, and the Word was with God, and the Word was God (John 1:1).

The Lord possessed me in the beginning of His way, before His works of old (Proverbs 8:22).

That which was from the beginning, which we have heard, which we have seen with our eyes, which we have looked upon, and our hands have handled, of the Word of life; (For the life was manifested, and we have seen it, and bear witness, and shew unto you that eternal life, which was with the Father, and was manifested unto us) (1 John 1:1-2).

Then I was by Him, as one brought up with Him: and I was daily His delight, rejoicing always before Him (Proverbs 8:30).

And now, O Father, glorify Thou Me with Thy own self with the glory which I had with Thee before the world was (John 17:5).

For there are three that bear record in heaven, the Father, the Word, and the Holy Ghost: and these three are one (1 John 5:7).

In the beginning God created the heaven and the earth (Genesis 1:1).

Introduction

In the Image of God...

The Bible tells us that God made man in His image, after His likeness (see Gen. 1:26-27). It also says that God breathed into man's nostrils the breath of life and that man became a living soul (see Gen. 2:7). Those statements assure me that although I am made of the ground, my movements, my very being, and my purpose for living are in God's likeness and of His nature.

As Jesus lived on this earth among us He provided us with an example of how to live. God's very nature was manifested in His daily action. This is also made possible for us through Jesus. We too can experience the fullness of the life and nature of God that Jesus expressed.

In order to understand the nature of God, who we are in Christ, what we have in Him, and what is available to us through Him, it is first necessary to investigate who Jesus Christ was and how He expressed the very nature of God. It is also important to understand who God is and what are the divine attributes by which He would have us to know and experience Him.

Elohim…Jehovah…El Shaddai…Adonai… One day I found myself wondering why God had so many names. When I asked Him, He responded, "David, those names describe the relationship that I desire to have with you and with all My people. Each name represents a different aspect of My personality and provision for you." So I began to study the names of God. Then God revealed something extraordinary to me. He said, "Your self image will be complete when you realize the complete image of who I want to be in you!" All that He is and has ever been, every dimension of His amazing personality, waits to reach fulfillment in you to complete your image!

By the end of this study, I hope you will see the impact of having been made in the image of God; that you will understand the divine attributes of God's image and the relationship He desires to have with you; and that you will see Jesus Christ not only as Savior, Redeemer, and God, but also as your model for the expression of God's image and nature in human flesh. You will be on your way to a walk with Him that is more flourishing and fruitful than you could have ever imagined.

Chapter 1

Elohim

The very first title of God that you encounter in the Bible is *Elohim*. It is the name that identifies God even before the beginning of time.

In the beginning God [Elohim] *created the heaven and the earth* (Genesis 1:1).

This fascinating name for God is one of the more frequently occurring titles in the Bible. It is used over 2,500 times! The root of *Elohim* is *El.* El refers to the "most high" God. Although comprised of only two letters, this small word describes God's greatness and glory, His power, and His sovereignty.

God of Creation

The name *Elohim* extends the scope of El's root meaning. It refers to the creative person of the most high God. Elohim demonstrates a new dimension of the God of power, for in it He becomes the God who creates! Two aspects of God are conveyed by the name *Elohim* thus far:

1

1. Complete sovereignty, power, and might.
2. Complete creativity.

God is shown as the Creator in the very first verse of the Bible! Through the name *Elohim*, Genesis 1:1 makes the statement that *tremendous, unimaginable power* is involved in the force of God's creativity. Elohim, in His mighty power and awesome creativity, caused our vast and exciting universe to come to exist simply from the words of His mouth.

Through faith we understand that the worlds were framed by the word of God, so that things which are seen were not made of things which do appear (Hebrews 11:3).

The Creative Trinity

As we marvel at the vastness and great variety of this great universe God spoke into being, we only begin to understand the creative potency of the name *Elohim*. Another startling characteristic of this name makes it even more distinctive. The Hebrew ending of Elohim is plural. From the very beginning, Scripture describes the divine Trinity of the Godhead—Father, Son, and Holy Spirit. No singular word could adequately describe this element of God's personality.

Several places throughout the Bible confirm this plurality. Genesis 1 says this about the creation of the first man, Adam:

*And God said, Let **Us** make man in **Our** image, after **Our** likeness: and let them have dominion over the fish*

*of the sea, and over the fowl of the air, and over the cat-
tle, and over all the earth, and over every creeping
thing that creepeth upon the earth. So God created
man in His own image, in the image of God created
He him; male and female created He them* (Genesis
1:26-27).

God the Father, Jesus the Son, and the Holy Spirit
were all involved in the creative process described in
Genesis 1. Genesis 1:1 shows that the Holy Spirit was
present. Genesis 1:2 shows that the Spirit of God
moved upon the face of the waters. And Genesis 1:3
tells us what was said: "And God said, Let there be
light...."

Why was the Holy Spirit moving upon the face of
the waters? Because He was preparing to create!

Jesus was also an active and present part of Creation:

*For by Him were all things created, that are in heaven,
and that are in earth, visible and invisible, whether
they be thrones, or dominions, or principalities, or pow-
ers: all things were created by Him, and for Him* (Co-
lossians 1:16).

*In the beginning was the Word, and the Word was
with God, and the Word was God. ... All things were
made by Him; and without Him was not any thing
made that was made. ... And the Word was made flesh
and dwelt among us, (and we beheld His glory, the
glory as of the only begotten of the Father,) full of grace
and truth* (John 1:1,3,14).

From the beginning of creation we see Elohim—Father, Son, and Holy Spirit—full of creative, sovereign power.

This increases the impact of Jesus' shocking statement to the religious men of His day, "Before Abraham was, I am" (Jn. 8:58b). With that statement Jesus declared Himself to be one with the creative God of the universe.

What an exciting, infinite personality! As an analogy, we can picture God as our *architect*; Jesus as the *building*; and the Holy Spirit as He who *breathes the life of God* into the structure. All creation points to Elohim—those who are mighty and powerful, those who are creative and sovereign.

God of Sustaining Power and Might

Yet there is an additional facet to the Elohim that keeps Him an active part of His creation. It is Elohim who makes covenants with those He created. Elohim is the name through which God reveals His power, the very power and creativity that allows God to enter into covenant relationship with us, His created beings. This was one of His purposes for creating us in the beginning.

The apostle Paul had a revelation of Elohim:

For I am not ashamed of the gospel of Christ: for it is the power of God unto salvation to every one that believeth; to the Jew first, and also to the Greek (Romans 1:16).

What Paul is saying in this verse of Scripture is that he found out that God's covenant of salvation for us— the image of Himself—is now more than His might and power! Don't ever speak lightly of the gospel, God's covenant with you and me, for that covenant is His power that gives us renewed life. It is His power that restores us, you and me, to life eternal through Jesus His Son. It is His power that saves us! Our covenant-making Elohim sustains all that He created through His might and power.

God's Judgment and Preserving Power

Naturally, Elohim loved His creation. He desired to preserve it. Although God was protective toward the people of His creation, He desired His creation to choose relationship with Him. Adam and Eve chose to sin in the garden and the generations that followed them seemed only to get "better and better at becoming worse and worse"!

Elohim is a mighty, perfect, righteous Creator. Everything as He created it was "very good" (Gen. 1:31). As we sin, however, we separate ourselves further and further from our Creator. Although God is merciful, sin was (and still is) offensive to Him. Something had to be done before we destroyed ourselves. Elohim observed this sinfulness growing and spreading like wild cancer through the generations that followed Adam and Eve.

Before long God began to notice a man named Enoch. Now Enoch wasn't necessarily outstanding in his hunger for God when God first noticed him, for his life was fairly uneventful until he reached the age of 65. Then something happened that turned his life around. Enoch's wife bore a child, and God told Enoch, "Name that baby *Methuselah*, which means, 'I have had enough of this sinfulness, so when this child dies, the flood will come upon the earth.' "

Surely no child received greater tender loving care than Methuselah, especially with the risk of an early death of the world hovering above his parents! However, in the days of Enoch nothing like our modern medicine was available. Death was a frequent visitor, and it frequently took small babies and young children who lacked resistance to disease. I can imagine Enoch's shock: "If this baby dies, judgment will come and totally destroy the earth. Wife, let's take good care of him!" As Enoch lovingly cared for Methuselah, something began to happen within him. Enoch's heart began to respond to his Creator, and Enoch began to serve the Lord.

The Bible tells us that for 300 years Enoch built a relationship with God. He walked with God and increased in his faith. Finally something extremely powerful took place; "...Enoch walked with God: and he was not; for God took him" (Gen. 5:24). (A surface reading of this statement may entice us to believe that Enoch simply vanished, but that was not the case.) One day Enoch was going about his usual routine, increasing in faith, when all of a sudden, God just reached down and carried him out of this life and into life eternal!

By faith Enoch was translated that he should not see death; and was not found, because God had translated him: for before his translation he had this testimony, that he pleased God (Hebrews 11:5).

Translate means "to carry across; to move out of sight." Enoch was translated by faith as he walked with God.

Meanwhile, Methuselah was still alive, growing older while the people around him continued to ignore the statement God had made. Methuselah's family probably kept people on pins and needles, for they knew the day was coming when the floods would arrive. Although Enoch walked closely with God, the same thing cannot be said about the other people of his generation. Their sinfulness vexed God continually. Yet Methuselah lived longer than any other person recorded in the Bible—969 years! His life was tremendously long for one reason: God kept extending His mercy and grace, hoping to preserve His creation. He loved those people He had created and did not want to destroy them.

Methuselah had a child named Lamech, and one of Lamech's sons was Noah. Notice the preservation of Enoch's family line. When you enter into a covenant with God, His promises are unto your seed and their seed and to as many as the Lord God shall call (see Acts 2:39).

Obedience Brings Reward

God had warned mankind of His coming judgment at the birth of Methuselah. Enoch prophesied to his generation regarding the approaching judgment of God. Yet the people still rebelled against God and refused to turn away from their wickedness.

Finally God spoke to Noah about His intentions for mankind:

...The end of all flesh is come before Me; for the earth is filled with violence through them; and, behold, I will destroy them with the earth (Genesis 6:13).

God proceeded to give Noah directions for building the ark, and Noah obeyed. Over the years, people had begun to take God's warning for granted. I would have thought that when Noah started to build the ark they'd have said, "Oh no! Methuselah is growing old, and God is preparing to send that flood He warned us about!" However, the people did the complete opposite. They scoffed at Noah. They had almost a thousand years in which to repent. Yet in spite of Noah's proclaiming of God's intentions to them, they rebelled. God always warns His people ahead of time when judgment is coming. He wants to give everyone a chance to repent.

Noah had tremendous faith, especially considering the fact that rain had never fallen upon the earth before! Noah built the ark to meet God's specifications, and it took 120 years to accomplish it. Just imagine having people harass you for that long. He could have stopped and said, "God, this is ridiculous! I mean, I've never seen rain before, and You have me out here preaching that there is going to be a flood. I quit!" But

Noah didn't give up. He held fast to the confidence of God's Word and kept building. Scripture tells us,

> *Cast not away therefore your confidence, which hath great recompense of reward. For ye have need of patience, that, after ye have done the will of God, ye might receive the promise* (Hebrews 10:35-36).

The reward that Noah received for his patience was very big. He finished the will of God! He and his family were spared. The seed parts of the earth were also saved so that they too could be replenished. In the flood the Elohim of creation destroyed His creation, which had become corrupted by the sin of mankind, yet Elohim also fulfilled His covenant with Enoch and Noah by preserving Noah and his family in the ark.

When God calls you to do something, don't quit. Remember that God is always faithful to fulfill His promises to those who do His will. God could have said, "I have had it. I am destroying this whole earth," but He didn't. Noah could have quit very easily, but he didn't. And you should never give up because you too have been created in God's image and God doesn't give up.

After having completed God's will, Noah and his family were spared. When the flood was over and the ark rested upon the top of Mount Ararat, God showed Himself again to Noah as Elohim, the God who makes covenants. God first spoke as Jehovah, the personal, authoritative, eternal God, and told Noah to make a sacrifice unto Him. Noah brought forth the animals and obeyed, making a sweet smelling sacrifice unto the Lord. Then something beautiful happened.

And God spake unto Noah, and to his sons with him, saying, and I, behold, I establish My covenant with you, and with your seed after you. ... And I will establish My covenant with you; neither shall all flesh be cut off any more by the waters of a flood; neither shall there any more be a flood to destroy the earth. ...This is the token of the covenant which I make between Me and you and every living creature that is with you, for perpetual generations: I do set My bow in the cloud, and it shall be for a token of a covenant between Me and the earth. ...and the waters shall no more become a flood to destroy all flesh (Genesis 9:8-9,11-13,15).

Elohim has shown Himself in two ways: He created a rainbow by His mighty power and He made a covenant with Noah that the rainbow was the sign of His promise to never again destroy the earth by flood. The rainbow should still remind you and me of the same covenant. Our mighty and powerful God dearly desires to protect His creation. So when you see a rainbow, think of Elohim! Think of this mighty, creative God who enters into everlasting agreements with His people!

God's Covenant People

Genesis 12 records the covenant God made with Abraham (while he was still called Abram). When God first spoke to Abraham, He used two names, *Jehovah* and *Elohim*.

Now the Lord had said unto Abram, Get thee out of thy country, and from thy kindred, and from thy father's house, unto a land that I will shew thee: and I will make of thee a great nation, and I will bless thee, and make thy name great; and thou shalt be a blessing: and I will bless them that bless thee, and curse him that curseth thee: and in thee shall all families of the earth be blessed (Genesis 12:1-3).

In this, God revealed Himself to Abraham as a God of blessing! He spoke in authority as Jehovah. We will study the name *Jehovah* later. The following verses will allow you to differentiate God as Jehovah from God as Elohim, the covenant God of power and might:

And Abram said, Lord God, what wilt Thou give me, seeing I go childless, and the steward of my house is this Eliezer of Damascus? And Abram said, Behold, to me Thou hast given no seed: and, lo, one born in my house is mine heir. And, behold, the word of the Lord came unto him, saying, This shall not be thine heir; but he that shall come forth out of thine own bowels shall be thine heir. And He brought him forth abroad, and said, Look now toward heaven, and tell the stars, if thou be able to number them: and He said unto him, So shall thy seed be (Genesis 15:2-5).

When Abram said, "Lord, God," he was saying, "I know Your ways, for You have revealed them to me, but I want a covenant with You. For only You are able to give me a child." It is in this same chapter that Elohim makes His covenant with Abram. When God first spoke to Abram, He commanded him to do three things. However, in the beginning Abram obeyed only two of the commandments he was given. He was given the following instructions:

1. Leave your country;
2. Leave your relatives;
3. Travel to the land to which God will lead you.

Obedience Brings Focus for Covenant

Abraham did leave his country for the land of promise, but he did one thing wrong—he took relatives with him. Accompanying Abram was his nephew Lot, as well as his father Terah (*Terah* literally means "delay"). This lack of obedience really was a big delay for Abram. God wanted to make a covenant with Abram, who was to become the "father of faith," but He could not make the agreement while Abram's eyes were on his family instead of Him.

On the way to the land of promise, Terah, who was very old and tired, needed to stop. Abram, Lot, and Terah halted their journey at a place called Haran, a name that means "dry and parched." There they stayed for about two years until Terah died.

God had told Abram, "Don't take your relatives." But because Abram did things his own way, he ended up in a dry, parched place where he couldn't hear from God. We are to love, honor, and obey our parents; this is a commandment from God Himself (see Eph. 6:1-2). But we are not to put our earthly relatives over the Word of God! That's when trouble comes. Let God have the very first place in your life. When you do, your spiritual walk will never become dry and parched; it will always be refreshing.

Because Abram's delay lasted about two years, when he reached the promised land there was a famine going on. Imagine how discouraging it must have been for him after delaying two years in the desert to reach his destination and find things weren't any better there! Also, he hadn't heard the voice of God for almost two years. I can imagine he wondered if he would ever hear it again.

Often we wonder why God rarely speaks to us when we haven't yet obeyed His first instructions. Silence may be God's way of saying, "You haven't finished what I asked you to do. When you fully obey My first words, I'll speak to you again—but not until then!" It took Abram a while to get the hint.

Now in the land of promise, Abram built an altar between Bethel and *Hai*, which means "a place of ruin." The altar should have been built in *Bethel*, meaning "the house of God." But Abram was just beginning to walk by faith, so perhaps he wasn't quite ready to build in Bethel yet.

The major activity Abram concerned himself with during his lifetime was building altars. He was a man who communed regularly with God. He highly esteemed the God of covenant and might. One really positive aspect of Abram's life story is that, although there were delays, "God always overcame them." So you see, God is bigger than the delays we put in our life! We should allow ourselves to be encouraged by the accounts of these men of faith who paved our way. We have the opportunity to learn from their mistakes and to be encouraged by how God divinely overcame the flaws of their humanity.

After building the altar between Bethel and Hai, Abram and his wife Sarai took Lot and travelled to Egypt to escape the famine. When they returned, Abram's altar had been destroyed, so he rebuilt it. Then Abram took his family and moved to a place called *Mamie*, which means "fatness," and to *Hebron*, which means "fellowship."

Apparently this was Abram's way of saying to all his delays, "Devil, you can try to destroy what I have built, but I will just build another altar and another and another. As long as I live, I will build."

Abram's new altar is significant because it shows that his communion with God was flourishing. However, Abram was still struggling with unbelief concerning God's promise about his descendants. He and Sarai still had not had any children. Abram probably thought, *Just in case I don't receive any children from God, I can raise my nephew Lot as my own child.* He was trying to play it safe just in case God didn't come through on His part of the bargain.

Eventually God had to *separate* Abram and Lot, and it turned out to be the best thing for them! They each had herdsmen who tended their flocks. Soon these herdsmen began to have great disagreements among themselves. One day Abram confronted Lot:

And Abram said unto Lot, Let there be no strife, I pray thee, between me and thee, and between my herdmen and thy herdmen; for we be brethren. Is not the whole land before thee? separate thyself, I pray thee, from me: if thou wilt take the left hand, then I will go to the right; or if thou depart to the right hand, then I will go to the left (Genesis 13:8-9).

Abram really exercised his godly qualities in this situation. He didn't say, "Well, Lot, since I'm older, you'd better honor me. I'll take the best portion of land." No! He said, "Lot, there are two sections of land, one to my right and one to my left." Many people who read this instantly think, *Abram was being humble; he didn't want to take the best for himself.* But that is not the case.

The truth is, Abram knew Elohim—God Almighty! Abram knew Elohim, the God who made covenants. It didn't matter to him which land Lot chose because he knew no matter where he lived God would protect him. By faith, Abram was saying, "It doesn't matter what my circumstances say. I know Elohim, and He rules over my circumstances!"

When Abram gave Lot the choice between lands, Lot looked around and immediately he saw two things:

And Lot lifted up his eyes, and beheld all the plain of Jordan, that it was well watered every where, before the Lord destroyed Sodom and Gomorrah, even as the garden of the Lord, like the land of Egypt, as thou comest unto Zoar (Genesis 13:10).

Then Lot said, "Abram, I'll take that nice, well-watered plain over there. You can have the mountainous region." Their decisions made, Lot and Abram separated. Abram and Sarai moved to the arid, mountainous area. And when they got there, what do you think happened? God spoke to Abram again!

Claiming the Promise

And the Lord said unto Abram, after that Lot was separated from him, Lift up now thine eyes, and look from the place where thou art northward, and southward, and eastward, and westward: for all the land which thou seest, to thee will I give it, and to thy seed for ever (Genesis 13:14-15).

It must have been very sweet for Abram to hear from God again. And finally, he knew the time was near to enter into a covenant with Almighty God. When Abram heard the covenant God spoke to him, he did not merely look around casually and say, "This, for me? Oh, God, how nice!"

The Bible tells us Abram lifted up his eyes! I believe he lifted up his eyes and received a vision, that he saw what God saw and it was a vision of faith! I believe when Abram looked northward, he saw the entire northern part of the Holy Land. Southward, Abram saw far, far beyond the mountain that blocked his view. Eastward and westward, what do you think Abram saw? He probably saw all the way to the Mediterranean Sea and over into Jordan! Now that Abram's relatives were out of the way, he could focus his eyes on God. But after God told Abram, "Lift up your eyes," He told him something else.

Arise, walk through the land in the length of it and in the breadth of it; for I will give it unto thee (Genesis 13:17).

A faith vision is not enough. You have to do more than just have a vision, you have to live it! You must walk it! Some people have a vision, but they do not have the action that goes with it. God told Abram, "You have to act on this vision! Walk through the land; I will give you the land that you tread upon."

I can imagine Abram being the world's first jogger. He jogged north, he jogged south, he jogged east, and he jogged west. I can imagine the Caananites talking as Abram jogged by, "Who is that man that just jogged down the road?" "I don't know, but I saw him going the other direction three days ago." Abram was running like a man who would possess the land. He was thinking of God's words, which said that his seed's seed would possess the land.

While running along, I'm sure Abram was saying, "This is mine; this is mine..." as he prepared himself to enter into a covenant relationship with God. Now when you stand on a faith claim, the devil will come to try to rob and steal and kill. So it is no surprise that something happened to Abram after he claimed this land!

It was not long until a wicked king named Cherdor-laomer roused up a group of other kings, and they came down from Elan (now Iran) with trouble on their minds. When they reached the cities of Sodom and Gomorrah, land upon which Abram had trod, they attacked. They carried off both people and possessions; they even took Lot captive, Abram's nephew.

Take heed; the devil will try to steal what you have claimed! When you claim something and tread upon the ground of God's work by speaking His promises, you had better prepare for battle. Some people stake their claims, but as soon as the enemy says, "You can't have it," they give up and lie down for dead! Of course the devil comes to steal. Jesus told you that he would (see Jn. 10:10), but you don't need to take it!

Abram wasn't about to play the enemy's game; he became really bold. Abram said, "They can't do this! I have trod upon this land, and it's mine. I won't put up with the enemy's tricks." I asked myself, *How could one man be so bold?* Then I realized, *It's because he knew Elohim, the God of covenant relationships.* Abram knew that God wouldn't give him land if He couldn't keep it. That land was for his seed's seed.

Abram banded together a group of his servants, and they went up to Elan and took everything back, *everything!* God is bigger, mightier, and more powerful than all the kings of history banded together. For God is the King of kings, and no man can do anything without Him (see Jn. 15:5). God knows how to take care of His

Creation, and He has done so for a long time. God knows how to take care of you. You must enter into a covenant relationship with Him. How do I know? Because by faith you are the seed of Abraham, and God told Abraham, "...Surely blessing I will bless thee, and multiplying I will multiply thee" (Heb. 6:14). He's a God who keeps His covenant. He is a God of might and power. He put Abram over in his situation and gave him might and power to win. He will give you might and power to win over your situation as well.

Strength to Receive the Promise

In the same day the Lord made a covenant with Abram, saying, Unto thy seed have I given this land, from the river of Egypt unto the great river, the river Euphrates: the Kenites, and the Kenizzites, and the Kadmonites, and the Hittites, and the Perizzites, and the Rephaims, and the Amorites, and the Canaanites, and the Girgashites, and the Jebusites (Genesis 15:18-21).

What would it take for Abram and Sarai to realize the impact of having a covenant with Almighty God? At this point, all they needed to realize was that they were supposed to have seed (children) and they still didn't have any. Abram must have thought, *It's going to take a lot of might and power to keep this covenant because my wife and I are far past our childbearing years!*

When Abram was 99 years old and Sarai was 89, God finally came and told them that they would have children. He also changed their names. *Abram* became

Abraham, which means "father of a multitude," and *Sarai* became *Sarah*, which means "princess of many nations." The Bible says that when God first changed Abram's name, he laughed out loud, for he couldn't believe that he was to become a father at his age (see Gen. 17:17). And when Sarai heard God telling Abram that he would have a child, she laughed too. When Abram's divine visitor said, "Sarai laughed," she was so embarrassed that she denied it (see Gen. 18:12-15).

They did have a child, and God prenamed the child *Isaac*, meaning "laughter." Abram and Sarai may have had the first laugh, but God had the last laugh! Hebrews 11 speaks of Isaac's birth. It tells us Sarah received the strength to have that child by faith. It took more than Abraham's faith to have seed; Abraham and Sarah had to be in agreement with God! The word for *strength* in the Greek is *dunamis*, or "miracle-working power." Where did the miracle-working power come from? It came from Elohim, the God of might and power!

We need to have a renewed image of the God of might and power, the God who is more than able to put us over in any of our difficulties! If God is for you, who can possibly be against you? No one! (See Romans 8:31.) Elohim is more powerful than anyone or anything that exists, and He is on our side. God wants us to rely on Him as our source of power and might. He wants to be Elohim *to* us, *in* us, *for* us right now, no matter what our current circumstances may be. Please, let

Him. Allow Him to renew your Spirit, your mind, your body, your emotions, and your image. From now on, as you study the Bible, every time you see the word *God* think, *Elohim, the God of might and power.* Then say to yourself, "He is my God! Praise the Lord!"

Elohim Revealed in the Word

Here are some Scriptures that refer to God as Elohim. When you need His power and might at work in your life read them and refresh your vision of His covenant with you, but don't wait until you're in a crisis! Before a crisis is the best time to read and be refreshed in the Word of Elohim.

I will say of the Lord, He is my refuge and my fortress: my God, in Him will I trust. Surely He shall deliver thee from the snare of the fowler, and from the noisome pestilence. He shall cover thee with His feathers, and under His wings shalt thou trust: His truth shall be thy shield and buckler (Psalm 91:2-4).

And they shall be My people, and I will be their God: and I will give them one heart, and one way, that they may fear Me for ever, for the good of them, and of their children after them: and I will make an everlasting covenant with them, that I will not turn away from them, to do them good; but I will put My fear in their hearts, that they shall not depart from Me (Jeremiah 32:38-40).

And [Solomon] *said, Lord God of Israel, there is no God like Thee, in heaven above, or on earth beneath, who keepest covenant and mercy with Thy servants that walk before Thee with all their heart* (1 Kings 8:23).

Be merciful unto me, O God, be merciful unto me: for my soul trusteth in Thee: yea, in the shadow of Thy wings will I make my refuge, until these calamities be overpast. I will cry unto God most high; unto God that performeth all things for me. He shall send from heaven, and save me from the reproach of him that would swallow me up. Selah. God shall send forth His mercy and His truth (Psalm 57:1-3).

Chapter 2

Jehovah

The name *Jehovah* is derived from the Hebrew word *Chavah*, meaning "to live." The name Jehovah is literally full of life! Jehovah is the self-existent or eternal name for God. It is rendered in the King James Version of the Bible as *Lord,* and it means "being" or "to be." We looked at God as *Elohim*, God of power and might. Now we will learn of Him as *Jehovah*, "the revealing one"! These names of God bring Him forth in a very personal way and describe the essence of our present tense God.

When Adam and Eve talked with God in the garden of Eden, they didn't talk with Him as Jehovah. At that time there had not yet been a separation of man from God, so Adam and Eve knew God as Elohim their Creator.

God Desires to Reveal Himself to You

Has the Lord ever spoken to you? God has often spoken to me through the divine revelation of His

Spirit. Sweet and precious is the communication between God's Spirit and ours. When He speaks to you, you will know it is Jehovah, the Revealing One.

He once characterized this wonderful side of His personality to me as I was praying. I said, "Lord, it's such a privilege to be restored with You." He responded, "David, you are not only restored with Me; you are also resurrected in Me." At this statement, my spirit became very excited!

Jehovah makes Himself known to you as your intimate, personal God. He walks with you, and He will never leave you nor forsake you (see Heb. 13:5b). The more you grow in your relationship with Him, the more of Himself He will reveal to you. Jehovah also denotes the unchanging nature of God. In Him there is "no variableness, neither shadow of turning" (Jas. 1:17). Psalm 102:27 reads, "But Thou art the same, and Thy years shall have no end." Jehovah is the One who is now and always has been. He is the God of life, the God of eternity!

Jehovah Chose Moses to Reveal Himself to His People

In our study of this name, we will study the life of Moses as recorded for us in the Book of Exodus. Moses was called by God to deliver His people out of Egypt and out of bondage (slavery). Moses' family was aware of his calling, and they were a family of faith. However, they were enslaved to the Egyptians along with the rest of the Israelites. Yet through miraculous circumstances, Moses grew up in Pharaoh's palace, and he was trained to be the next pharaoh. This is quite a comfortable set of circumstances, wouldn't you say?

To the natural eye, it probably looked to Moses' parents as if he could not possibly be the deliverer of the Hebrews. After all, he had it made, why would he want to deliver the Israelites from the hand of the Egyptians? We need to realize that if God wants us to do something, He will deal with us until He gets us right where He wants us! So God dealt with Moses. At 40 years of age, Moses finally decided that since God had called him to deliver the Israelites, he may as well get on with it.

Have you ever tried to help God? I know we all have from time to time, and that's what Moses did. When he saw an Egyptian beating one of the Israelites, Moses lost his temper and went out and killed the Egyptian. That created a problem for Moses. When the Egyptians found out about this affair, they were furious. Moses had to flee for his life. Not only that, but undoubtedly the Israelites also suffered dearly because of Moses' action. So they became enraged at Moses as well.

Moses fled to a place called Midian (a desert place). He lived there in the desert tending sheep for 40 years. I've often wondered about what he did during those 40 years. Some Bible scholars think he wrote the Book of Job during this time, and he very well could have. Some suggest that he wrote Genesis here; others feel Genesis was written on Mount Sinai with the rest of the Pentateuch.

God orchestrated all the experiences Moses had out there in the desert because Moses was to later lead God's people through the desert. After living there for 40 years, Moses probably knew all about the desert. Certainly Moses also knew all about sheep and leadership, for people can be a lot like sheep. If you give Him half an opportunity Jehovah will use everything in your life and use it for His glory.

I'm sure Moses didn't expect God to turn his situation into a glorious one. In fact, I believe he lost confidence that God would ever use him again. But God plays until He wins; and when God wins, He wants to make you a winner too! Every time you win, it credits God. In fact, every victory in your past credited God—whether you were walking with Him or not.

The apostle Paul said it so well:

Now thanks be unto God, which always causeth us to triumph in Christ... (2 Corinthians 2:14).

God Wants His People to Win

God wanted Moses to win, and He had set some high goals for Moses. God has high goals for the lives of each of His people. Don't get jealous of other Christians when they do well, for you're a part of the same Body of Christ. Instead of feeling jealous, support your brothers and sisters in Christ; tell them, "When you are doing well, so am I because we're a part of the same Body!" Success is a credit to God's Kingdom! Moses didn't have anyone around to stimulate his faith the way we can do for each other. So God, whether Moses was aware of it or not, stepped into the scene with every intention of turning him into a winner.

One day Moses was tending sheep near a place called Mount Horeb, which means "fresh inspiration." (This mountain is also known as Mount Sinai.) Now after 40 years of tending sheep in the wilderness, God was ready to give Moses fresh inspiration. Have you ever felt like you have been in the wilderness for 40 years? God can give you fresh inspiration, even if you think you have already blown it. He will always pick you up, and He will never put you down!

Moses was simply tending his sheep when all of a sudden a burning bush near the top of the mountain caught his eye. What was particularly unique about this fire was that it was not consuming the bush. So Moses set out to see what was going on. What do you think was on Moses' mind? He probably wondered, *Who or what could it be for a fire to act like that?* As he approached the burning bush the fire continued to burn its unconsuming flame.

And when the Lord saw that he turned aside to see, God called unto him out of the midst of the bush, and said, Moses, Moses. And he said, Here am I. And He said, Draw not nigh hither: put off thy shoes from off thy feet, for the place whereon thou standest is holy ground (Exodus 3:4-5).

What a shock! I don't think Moses expected to hear the voice of the Lord.

And the Lord said, I have surely seen the affliction of My people which are in Egypt, and have heard their cry by reason of their taskmasters; for I know their sorrows; and I am come down to deliver them out of the hand of the Egyptians, and to bring them up out of that land unto a good land and a large, unto a land flowing with milk and honey; unto the place of the Canaanites, and the Hittites, and the Amorites, and the Perizzites, and the Hivites, and the Jebusites (Exodus 3:7-8).

God was saying, "Moses, you're the man I want to use to deliver My people." Now, imagine Moses saying, "God, I am 80 years old! If you would had asked me 40 years ago I would have said, 'I am your deliverer,' but, God, *now*? You mean now?! Who am I? I've blown it so badly!" After Moses had spent 40 years with those sheep God was telling him, "You are ready to deliver My sheep."

God majors in creating winners! He said, "I will be with you and give you a token of My presence, Moses. You will go back and lead My people out of Egypt. Then you will return to this mountain and serve Me." Moses said, "When I go to deliver the children of Israel, they are going to ask me Your name, and I don't even know it!" God told him, "You just tell them that *I AM* sent you." Who is I AM? That's Jehovah, the One who revealed Himself to the children of Israel.

Jehovah was not only revealing Himself to the Israelites; He was also revealing His plan to deliver them from the Egyptians and lead them into the promised land. God didn't want Moses to limit Him to one name. He planned to be *all* that the children of Israel would need, so He was saying, "I AM"—I shall be everything you need.

> *And God said unto Moses, I AM THAT I AM: and He said, Thus shalt thou say unto the children of Israel, I AM hath sent me unto you. And God said moreover unto Moses, Thus shalt thou say unto the children of Israel, The Lord God of your fathers, the God of Abraham, the God of Isaac, and the God of Jacob, hath sent me unto you: this is My name for ever, and this is My memorial unto all generations* (Exodus 3:14-15).

Here God was revealing Himself as Jehovah, the One who is the same yesterday, today, and forever (see Heb. 13:8). He was saying, "I am Abraham's God, Isaac's God, Jacob's God, and I am your God! Generations change, but I don't change, Moses."

God Is Persistent in His Call

God revealed to Moses that he was to be the person who would deliver the Israelites from the hand of the Egyptians. But even though God was full of good plans, Moses was full of excuses. Do you see Moses' attitude in yourself? Moses said, "The elders of Israel aren't going to listen to this." So God said, "What's that in your hand?" "It's a rod, Lord." God said, "Throw it down on the ground." When Moses cast it to the ground, it became a serpent and Moses fled from it. God said, "Don't run from it, Moses, pick it up." Moses picked up the serpent, and immediately it was a rod in Moses' hand again! (See Exodus 4:1-5.)

Even though God told Moses, "I will give you that sign for the elders and for Pharaoh," Moses still had a lack of trust. He just couldn't imagine himself as much of a deliverer. Then God said, "If that isn't enough, Moses, I'll give you another sign."

And the Lord said furthermore unto him, Put now thine hand into thy bosom. And he put his hand into his bosom: and when he took it out, behold, his hand was leprous as snow. And He said, Put thine hand into thy bosom again. And he put his hand into his bosom again; and plucked it out of his bosom, and, behold, it was turned again as his other flesh (Exodus 4:6-7).

The first time Moses withdrew his hand from his heart, it was leprous. God was telling him, "Moses, when you killed that Egyptian man, you were acting out of the wrong motive to deliver. You were trying to deliver by yourself, and you didn't follow Me. For I, Jehovah, had not yet revealed Myself to you. When you put your hand on your heart the second time, your hand will be clean just like your spiritual motive." Now when Moses went forth to deliver, signs would accompany his actions.

God was overcoming Moses' arguments, but Moses was still holding out. He said, "Lord, I just can't do it. I don't speak well enough." When Moses made this statement, I can imagine the Lord saying, "Moses, that's not true." This is confirmed by Acts 7:22, which says that Moses was "mighty in words and in deeds." Having been raised up with the best of Egyptian training in Pharaoh's court, Moses had been schooled for eloquent public speaking. How many of us who are in Christ shortchange ourselves by trying to shortchange God? By not spending time in the Spirit, we will always come short of God's will in what He wants us to do and where He wants us to be. Perhaps Moses' exile in the desert had given him a bad self-image. Nevertheless, God was fed up with Moses' excuses!

And the Lord said unto him, Who hath made man's mouth? or who maketh the dumb, or deaf, or the seeing, or the blind? have not I the Lord? Now therefore go, and I will be with thy mouth, and teach thee what thou shalt say (Exodus 4:11-12).

"Who made your mouth anyway?" What a powerful reply! Jehovah had to remind Moses that He is also Elohim, the powerful Creator. Then He said to Moses, "Look, if you are going to drag your feet about this, we'll get Aaron, your brother, to speak for you. Besides, all the men who sought your life are dead, so you don't have a thing to worry about." That stripped away Moses' last excuse. He probably thought that he would be facing people who wanted his head. (You see, when we have sin in our life, fear rules us.)

Jehovah won Moses over by bringing him out of the dark about his past. As it turned out, Aaron didn't do any speaking to the Pharaoh; Moses did it all. After all, when the Lord God is on your side, who else do you need? When Moses arrived in Egypt and began to speak His word, God gave tremendous demonstrations of His power as Elohim. God also revealed Himself as Jehovah, I AM, and mighty works followed.

Jehovah Shows Himself Mightier Than the Gods of Egypt

Every plague God sent upon Egypt was a judgment against one of the idols the Egyptians worshiped. For example, they worshiped frogs, represented by a god called Heki and mummified frogs, so God said, "You like frogs? I'll give you more frogs than you can ever imagine!" After that there were frogs everywhere the Egyptians lived. The Egyptians worshiped the Nile River, and God turned it to blood, the Nile and all the waters in Egypt. The Egyptians also worshiped a sun god named Ra, so God plagued the land with darkness. The interesting feature of this darkness was that it was discriminating, for it was only dark in Egypt. Over in Goshen where the Israelites lived light still shone.

Elohim is a God who desires to redeem and restore sinners. By the clear discriminating nature of the plagues Pharaoh suspected something was up. I believe God was trying to win the Egyptians over to Him, as well as the Israelites, for He loves sinners too. Those mighty signs were God's way of saying to the Egyptians, "Your idols are wrong. I AM your Creator Elohim, God of power and might. I AM Jehovah. I AM all that you need. Turn to Me."

Finally, Pharaoh's heart was changed, and he set the children of Israel free. I think a lot of Egyptians were also won over because the Bible says that a "mixed multitude" followed Moses out of Egypt into the wilderness (Ex. 12:38).

God's evidence of Himself as Jehovah was still to be seen. God took good care of His people. Their shoes and garments didn't wear out, and He provided them with free heating in the cold and air conditioning in the heat. A cool cloud covered and led them by day, and a pillar of fire by night. The cloud kept them shielded from the desert heat in the daytime, and the pillar of fire kept them warm at night in the desert cold.

God is the General of generals! He even acted as their military protection. Who else would part a body of water so that an entire people could pass through without being harmed? But how easily the Israelites seemed to forget. It wasn't long before the children of Israel began murmuring, and that didn't go over well with God or Moses. Exodus chapters 14 and 15 describe many of the Israelites' experiences as they sojourned through the wilderness and arrived at Mount Horeb (Mount Sinai), where Moses had first heard God's voice from the burning bush.

God Reveals His Righteousness

God took Moses to the mountaintop and began to speak to him, and gave him the ten commandments. I also believe that this is where God revealed Genesis to Moses. Moses wasn't just sitting idly on top of Mount

Horeb for 40 days and nights, despite the fact that a lot of people think you just go in the presence of God and do nothing more than just sit there resting in Him. I am sure God keeps Himself busy. But while Moses was up on the mountaintop, things weren't going well at all for the children of Israel. They didn't expect Moses to be gone that long. Maybe they thought he could just say, "Well, Lord, this is taking quite a while, and it's getting late. I have to get back to my people now." It doesn't work that way. But when the children of Israel became really restless, they rebelled.

And when the people saw that Moses delayed to come down out of the mount, the people gathered themselves together unto Aaron, and said unto him, Up, make us gods, which shall go before us; for as for this Moses, the man that brought us up out of the land of Egypt, we wot not what is become of him (Exodus 32:1).

When God heard and saw what the people were saying and doing, He became very angry. He said, "Moses, get down there! I'm disgusted with those people!"

In His righteous indignation, God revealed Himself as Jehovah. The Lord's personality is one of pure righteousness and holiness. Consider Leviticus 19:2, which says, "...Ye shall be holy: for I the Lord your God am holy." This literally means, "I, Jehovah, your Elohim am holy." It is Jehovah who must pronounce the judgment that condemns sin, and He was really ready to pronounce judgment against the children of Israel for worshiping the gods of Egypt!

God said, "Moses, you go tell your people that you brought out of Egypt that I will wipe them out. We'll start over again, and I will make you into a great nation." (Wait a minute! Are the Israelites really *Moses'* people? In Exodus 3:7 Jehovah had told Moses, "I have surely seen the affliction of My people....")

Now therefore let Me alone, that My wrath may wax hot against them, and that I may consume them: and I will make of thee a great nation. And Moses besought the Lord his God, and said, Lord, why doth Thy wrath wax hot against Thy people, which Thou hast brought forth out of the land of Egypt with great power, and with a mighty hand? (Exodus 32:10-11)

At this point Moses had been walking with Jehovah for perhaps a year. So he said, "God, You're the One who brought these people forth as Elohim, God of power, and they are not my people, they're Yours!" No one could talk to the Lord like that unless they knew Him really well. Moses was actually arguing with God, who had already said, "That's My decision, now leave Me alone!"

Then Moses said something very interesting:

Wherefore should the Egyptians speak, and say, For mischief did He bring them out, to slay them in the mountains, and to consume them from the face of the earth? Turn from Thy fierce wrath, and repent of this evil against Thy people (Exodus 32:12).

What an appeal for mercy! I can see Moses telling Jehovah, "If You kill these people, You will surely hurt

Your reputation, God. The Egyptians are going to say, 'Look at that God—He ain't too cool. He brought those people out into the desert and got mad at them, just like He did us. Then He killed them all.' " Moses was appealing to the Revealing One, but he wasn't finished yet:

> *Remember Abraham, Isaac, and Israel, Thy servants, to whom Thou swarest by Thine own self, and saidst unto them, I will multiply your seed as the stars of heaven, and all this land that I have spoken of will I give unto your seed, and they shall inherit it for ever* (Exodus 32:13).

Moses spoke God's Word, "God, what about Your promise to Abraham, Isaac, and Jacob? You said You'd make of their seed a great nation. If You destroy these people You won't be honoring Your Word." Now, what do you think Jehovah did? "And the Lord repented of the evil which He thought to do unto His people" (Ex. 32:14). Jehovah took the people back as His own. Why? Moses prayed the Word, and God saw that he magnified His Word about His name.

Moses descended the mountain carrying the tablets containing God's commandments. When he neared the bottom, he discovered why the Lord was so angry with His people. Throughout the camp there was noise, commotion, and people dancing, and there in the center of the camp sat a golden calf that the people were worshiping. Moses became angry. He was furious at their sin. (Moses probably got his attitude from Jehovah God who loves sinners but hates sin.)

Then Moses stood in the gate of the camp, and said, Who is on the Lord's side? let him come unto me. And all the sons of Levi gathered themselves together unto him (Exodus 32:26).

All of Moses' immediate family from the tribe of Levi came and stood with Moses.

And he said unto them, Thus saith the Lord God of Israel, Put every man his sword by his side, and go in and out from gate to gate throughout the camp, and slay every man his brother, and every man his companion, and every man his neighbour. And the children of Levi did according to the word of Moses: and there fell of the people that day about three thousand men (Exodus 32:27-28).

Moses' successful intercession with God to accept the people back to Himself did not mean that everything was a bed of roses again. Sin is still sin until it is forgiven. Moses gave all the people opportunity to repent. He had already argued their case with God. Then Moses went to the people and told them to stop sinning. Those who hardened their hearts were put to death. You would think, *Well, they had it tough. No one gets put to death for sinning in our days.* Well, guess what? Romans 8:6 says, "For to be carnally minded is death; but to be spiritually minded is life and peace."

An Intercessor Will Know God's Heart

Moses gave all of the people a chance to choose life, but only the sons of Levi made the right decision. After the unrighteous were slain, Moses went before Jehovah again and took a priestly stand.

And Moses returned unto the Lord, and said, Oh, this people have sinned a great sin, and have made them gods of gold. Yet now, if Thou wilt forgive their sin–; and if not, blot me, I pray thee, out of Thy book which Thou hast written (Exodus 32:31-32).

Do you want others to win, or do you just want to win yourself? If you really want to have a heart that flows with God's will, have a heart like Moses. He had favor with God because he spent valued time with God. He knew God's heart. And Moses used that favor to save his nation. Moses entered into his calling as a priest, and by doing so he entered into the personality of Jehovah Himself.

And the Lord said unto Moses, Whosoever hath sinned against Me, him will I blot out of My book. Therefore now go, lead the people unto the place of which I have spoken unto thee: behold, mine Angel shall go before thee: nevertheless in the day when I visit I will visit their sin upon them. And the Lord plagued the people, because they made the calf, which Aaron made (Exodus 32:33-35).

God still dealt with the people for their sin. Some people say, "I've repented, so everything is well." People who make this statement miss God's heart and intention. This is "greasy, greasy grace" and "joppy, sloppy agape." There is still a law that began in the beginning of Genesis that we must understand. It is the law of sowing and reaping. Some people (some Christians) want to make up their own rules as they go, but they cannot bend the law of God.

And the Lord said unto Moses, Depart, and go up hence, thou and the people which thou hast brought up out of the land of Egypt, unto the land which I sware unto Abraham, to Isaac, and to Jacob, saying, Unto thy seed will I give it: and I will send an angel before thee...for I will not go up in the midst of thee; for thou art a stiffnecked people: lest I consume thee in the way (Exodus 33:1-3).

God said, "I'll send an angel before you to bring you into the promised land, but I'm not going with you because I cannot stand your rebellion."

When the people heard that, they took off all their heathen ornaments and stood at the doorways of their tents. Moses went to the tabernacle and once again entered into his priestly role to commune with God. When Moses entered the tabernacle, the cloud descended upon the tabernacle. The children of Israel must have thought, *What a relief.*

And all the people saw the cloudy pillar stand at the tabernacle door: and all the people rose up and worshipped, every man in his tent door. And the Lord spake unto Moses face to face, as a man speaketh unto his friend. And he turned again into the camp: but his servant Joshua, the son of Nun, a young man, departed not out of the tabernacle. And Moses said unto the Lord, See, Thou sayest unto me, Bring up this people: and Thou hast not let me know whom Thou wilt send with me. Yet Thou hast said, I know thee by name, and thou hast also found grace in My sight (Exodus 33:10-12).

Moses was after God again! He was saying, "God, You haven't said which angel is going to take us into the promised land. Remember, God, You called me by name, and You gave me grace and favor in Your sight. If You won't go with us and consider this nation as Your people, we're not going at all!" Moses could have thought, *I've had it with this crowd of murmuring people*, but he didn't. Why could Moses talk with God in this way? Because he knew God as Jehovah! Moses had an intimate relationship with his Lord. And what did God say to him?

And He said, My presence shall go with thee, and I will give thee rest. And he said unto Him, If Thy presence go not with me, carry us not up hence (Exodus 33:14-15).

So God went with them. The presence of the Lord was promised by God, and His presence finally brought the people into rest.

But Moses was a spiritual opportunist, and God liked that quality. God doesn't have special people who He picks as pets. Some Christians get more because they stick with God and give all they have. God didn't turn Moses down when he became bold. God said this to Moses:

And he said, I beseech Thee, shew me Thy glory. And He said, I will make all My goodness pass before thee, and I will proclaim the name of the Lord before thee; and will be gracious to whom I will be gracious, and will shew mercy on whom I will shew mercy. And He said, Thou canst not see My face: for there shall no man see Me, and live. And the Lord said, Behold, there is a place by Me, and thou shalt stand upon a rock: and it shall come to pass, while My glory passeth by, that I will put thee in a cleft of the rock, and will cover thee with My hand while I pass by: and I will take away Mine hand, and thou shalt see My back parts: but My face shall not be seen (Exodus 33:18-23).

God gave Moses some of what he asked for. See, God knows what we can handle, and He will not give us any thing that will harm us. Why did God give this to Moses? He gave it because Moses was saying, "I want to see Your glory; I desire an even closer relationship with You, Jehovah!"

We Are Called to Know Him

God has wonderful things in store for those who desire a close walk with Him—like the relationship with Him that Moses had. When I read this Exodus 33, I see the Lord of love and my heart leaps. It really illustrates what God has done for you and me; He has called us to enter into His priesthood.

Jehovah didn't call us to condemn us. He called us to be reconciled with Him. He has called each and every one of us to a reconciled relationship with Him and to make the world a winning place! Jehovah has called us to go before Him in prayer and intercession:

"God, have mercy upon them! God, save them, for they are Your people. You have made Yourself to die for them all. Wax not towards us, but have mercy."

Our priestly calling toward the world is to tell all people about the name and mercy of the God of creation, Elohim, and Jehovah, who is an "always with you and in you" God. We need to share this because we want people to win; because we want them to have life and have it more abundantly (see Jn. 10:10).

When you take on the priestly calling of Jehovah—as we all should—the Lord who lives in you will reveal Himself to you and through you to others. Jehovah is a beautiful name, the Ever-Revealing One.

Zechariah prophesied, saying:

Sing and rejoice, O daughter of Zion: for, lo, I come, and I will dwell in the midst of thee, saith the Lord. And many nations shall be joined to the Lord in that day, and shall be My people: and I will dwell in the midst of thee, and thou shalt know that the Lord of hosts hath sent me unto thee (Zechariah 2:10-11).

Jehovah gave us insight and told us beforehand just what to look for from Him. Who was He talking about? Jesus! If you study Jehovah from one end of the Bible to the other, you will find that He is the Lord Jesus Christ, Jehovah, revealed to you!

Jehovah Reveals Himself Through His Word

If you need a special revelation of who Jehovah God is, read through these Scriptures that show Him as

Lord. Let Him, the personal, Ever-Revealing One in your life, fill you with the revelation of His redeeming mercy.

But the mercy of the Lord is from everlasting to everlasting upon them that fear Him, and His righteousness unto children's children (Psalm 103:17).

Tell ye, and bring them near; yea, let them take counsel together: who hath declared this from ancient time? who hath told it from that time? have not I the Lord? and there is no God else beside Me; a just God and a Saviour; there is none beside Me (Isaiah 45:21).

And I will bring the third part through the fire, and will refine them as silver is refined, and will try them as gold is tried: they shall call on My name, and I will hear them: I will say, It is My people: and they shall say, The Lord is my God (Zechariah 13:9).

The fear of the Lord is the beginning of knowledge: but fools despise wisdom and instruction. My son, hear the instruction of thy father, and forsake not the law of thy mother: for they shall be an ornament of grace unto thy head, and chains about thy neck (Proverbs 1:7-9).

O Lord, Thou hast searched me, and known me. Thou knowest my downsitting and mine uprising, Thou understandest my thought afar off. Thou compassest my path and my lying down, and art acquainted with all my ways. For there is not a word in my tongue, but, lo, O Lord, Thou knowest it altogether. Thou hast beset me behind and before, and laid Thine hand upon me (Psalm 139:1-5).

In the beginning was the Word, and the Word was with God, and the Word was God. The same was in the beginning with God. All things were made by Him; and without Him was not any thing made that was made. In Him was life; and the life was the light of men. And the light shineth in darkness; and the darkness comprehended it not. There was a man sent from God, whose name was John. The same came for a witness, to bear witness of the Light, that all men through him might believe. He was not that Light, but was sent to bear witness of that Light. That was the true Light, which lighteth every man that cometh into the world. He was in the world, and the world was made by Him, and the world knew Him not. He came unto His own, and His own received Him not. But as many as received Him, to them gave He power to become the sons of God, even to them that believe on His name: which were born, not of blood, nor of the will of the flesh, nor of the will of man, but of God. And the Word was made flesh, and dwelt among us, (and we beheld His glory, the glory as of the only begotten of the Father,) full of grace and truth (John 1:1-14).

For unto us a child is born, unto us a son is given: and the government shall be upon His shoulder: and His name shall be called Wonderful, Counsellor, The mighty God, The everlasting Father, The Prince of Peace. Of the increase of His government and peace there shall be no end, upon the throne of David, and upon His kingdom, to order it, and to establish it with judgment and with justice from henceforth even for ever. The zeal of the Lord [Jehovah] *of hosts will perform this* (Isaiah 9:6-7).

Afterward He brought me to the gate, even the gate that looketh toward the east: and, behold, the glory of the God of Israel came from the way of the east: and His voice was like a noise of many waters: and the earth shined with His glory. And it was according to the appearance of the vision which I saw, even according to the vision that I saw when I came to destroy the city: and the visions were like the vision that I saw by the river Chebar; and I fell upon my face. and the glory of the Lord came into the house by the way of the gate whose prospect is toward the east. So the spirit took me up, and brought me into the inner court; and, behold, the glory of the Lord [Jehovah] *filled the house. And I heard Him speaking unto me out of the house; and the man stood by me. And He said unto me, Son of man, the place of My throne, and the place of the soles of My feet, where I will dwell in the midst of the children of Israel for ever, and My holy name, shall the house of Israel no more defile, neither they, nor their kings, by their whoredom, nor by the carcases of their kings in their high places* (Ezekiel 43:1-7).

Should you have any problem seeing the truth about Jehovah in these Scriptures, keep in mind that we have a bearer of truth!

But all these things will they do unto you for My name's sake, because they know not Him that sent Me. If I had not come and spoken unto them, they had not had sin: but now they have no cloak for their sin. He that hateth Me [Jehovah] *hateth My Father* [Elohim] *also. If I had not done among them the works which none other man did, they had not had sin: but now have they both seen and hated both Me and My Father. But this cometh to pass, that the word might be fulfilled that is written in their law, They hated Me* [Jehovah] *without a cause. But when the Comforter is come, whom I will send unto you from the Father, even the Spirit of truth, which proceedeth from the Father, He shall testify of Me: and ye also shall bear witness, because ye have been with Me from the beginning* (John 15:21-27).

Chapter 3

El Shaddai

When we studied the name Elohim, we discovered that *El* conveys God's power and might. *El Shaddai* is another compound name. It first appears in Genesis 17.

And when Abram was ninety years old and nine, the Lord [Elohim] appeared to Abram, and said unto him, I am the Almighty God; walk before Me, and be thou perfect. And I will make My covenant between Me and thee, and will multiply thee exceedingly (Genesis 17:1-2).

Does "God Almighty" mean the same thing as "God of might and power"? No, it doesn't. The name *El Shaddai* bears a different meaning entirely. It means "to clarify, brighten, to make clean or purify, purge out, and chosen." Basically, this name is derived from the Hebrew word meaning *field*—like fields that produce abundance. It is also translated as "breast" or "the many breasted one," which signifies nourishment and productivity. In this sense, God is shown as the One who is more than enough. He is the One who is all sufficient!

When you see the name *El Shaddai*, God is saying, "I am more than enough to meet your needs in each situation."

God Provides in the Face of "Impossible" Circumstances

Throughout Abraham's life, God made promises to bless and multiply him. The Bible says that Abraham's blessings are also ours (see Gal. 3:14,27). As El Shaddai, God came to Abraham when things looked totally impossible. He came and said, "I will give you seed as the dust of the earth" (see Gen. 13:16).

When God finally announced that it would soon be time for Sarah to conceive Isaac, Abraham was 99 years old. If that's not an "impossible" enough situation, his wife was 89 years old. God showed His all sufficiency by turning nature around and providing a miracle that is contrary to natural processes. Even though God Himself set the course of nature in motion, He is more than capable of superseding all natural events! That is what happened when He caused Abraham and Sarah to have a child.

Abraham's son was named Isaac, and Isaac also knew God as El Shaddai. When Isaac's own son Jacob left home to find a wife, Isaac spoke to him.

And Isaac called Jacob, and blessed him, and charged him, and said unto him, Thou shalt not take a wife of the daughters of Canaan. Arise, go to Padanaram, to the house of Bethuel thy mother's father; and take thee a wife from thence of the daughters of Laban thy mother's brother. And God Almighty bless thee, and make thee fruitful, and multiply thee, that thou mayest be a multitude of people (Genesis 28:1-3).

Isaac was saying, "Jacob, may El Shaddai, the God who is all sufficient, bless you and multiply you! He will work contrary to nature to overcome any difficult circumstances." Jacob left home with his father's blessings and the birthright, but with nothing in his hand. In fact, he left behind an irate brother, whom he had cheated out of his birthright. The brother's name was Esau, and Esau was more than ready to kill Jacob. Jacob had always been a "Momma's boy," and as he left home he was entering a totally strange situation that didn't look prosperous at all.

On the way to Padanaram, Jacob fell asleep and dreamed of a ladder on which angels ascended and descended. Then God spoke to him: "I'm giving this land to you and your seed, and I will protect you" (see Gen. 28:11-15).

Greatly encouraged, Jacob continued on his way. When he arrived, he fell in love with a beautiful girl named Rachel. However, Rachel's father Laban didn't possess many beautiful qualities. Laban was tricky and mean. He promised Rachel to Jacob if he would work seven years for her, but when the time was up, he gave Leah, Rachel's older sister, to Jacob instead. Jacob then had to work another seven years in order to receive Rachel as his wife. To look at the situation, Jacob didn't seem very blessed. On top of all of this, Laban changed

Jacob's wages ten times, and he kept stealing Jacob's things (see Gen. 29:23-26). Jacob was in a horrible predicament. Finally, God spoke to him and said, "I want you to return to the promised land" (see Gen. 31:3).

Jacob may have thought, *Well, I will go back poor, but anything is better than living with Laban.* But El Shaddai, the God who is more than enough, intended to prosper him. Some people want everything right away—instant birth, instant growth, and instant result to prayer. But God is not an instant doer; He prepares you for what you pray for according to His will (see 1 Jn. 5:14). Prayer is confession to God that you know His will. You have to hold fast to your confidence in order to obtain rewards (see Jas. 5:7-8). You have to be patient and know that God is never late. Sometimes He's just in time, but He is never late. Last minute or not, hold fast to Him the way Jacob did and you won't miss the recompense of your reward.

God told Jacob, "I will bless and prosper you, if you will follow these instructions [if you follow Me]. When the cattle are taking water, where they usually mate, place speckled, spotted, and striped stakes in the ground. Let them watch the stakes, and you keep your eyes on them, too. Then, when they conceive, they will have speckled, spotted, and striped animals. Those animals will be yours." (See Genesis 30:31-32,38-39.)

Jacob told Laban, "For my hire, I want to take with me all of the speckled, spotted, and striped animals that are born. They will be mine when it is time for me to leave."

I'm sure Laban thought, *Great! There are hardly ever any of those.* He really regretted it later because it was not long until all the animals born were spotted, speckled, and striped! Jacob and his animals kept seeing those stakes. God set forth a vision to bring His Word to pass, and Jacob left Laban a very wealthy man. Why? Because the all-sufficient El Shaddai was in control. El Shaddai took hold of the natural things and turned them around into supernatural miracles. Jacob knew El Shaddai as did Isaac, his father, and Abraham, his grandfather.

Genesis 35 tells of a third vision Jacob had.

And God appeared unto Jacob again, when he came out of Padanaram, and blessed him. And God said unto him, Thy name is Jacob: thy name shall not be called any more Jacob, but Israel shall be thy name: and He called his name Israel. And God said unto him, I am God Almighty: be fruitful and multiply; a nation and a company of nations shall be of thee, and kings shall come out of thy loins (Genesis 35:9-11).

Jacob had lived in the midst of strange circumstances and strange people, but God said, "Your situation doesn't matter! I am what matters. Let Me turn your circumstances around and bless you!"

God brought Jacob out from Laban's household as a wealthy man, reconciled him with his once angry brother, Esau, and gave him many children. Jacob lived as a wealthy, blessed man to a ripe old age because he knew El Shaddai.

Almighty always relates to blessings and multiplication because that name speaks of more than enough. It speaks of abundances. When Jesus said, "I came to give you life, and to give it to you more abundantly" (see Jn. 10:10b), He was speaking as El Shaddai, our God who supplies nourishment for body, soul, and spirit in abundance.

Moses Experienced the Provision of El Shaddai

Moses also knew El Shaddai. God spoke to him this way in Exodus chapter 6:

And I appeared unto Abraham, unto Isaac, and unto Jacob, by the name of God Almighty [Elohim], but by My name Jehovah was I not known to them (Exodus 6:3).

God was telling Moses, "I appeared to them as a God who is more than enough, and I am speaking to you too." Scholars attribute Psalm 91 to Moses, who definitely learned the grace and provision of El Shaddai.

He that dwelleth in the secret place of the most High shall abide under the shadow of the Almighty (Psalm 91:1).

Moses extols the power of God that sheltered them from the plagues that were upon Egypt. In this verse, the word *dwelleth* actually means "to stake your claim." Just imagine this: he who stakes his claim in the secret place of the most High will abide under the shadow of the Almighty. Moses declared, "I'm staking my claim under the shadow of God who is more than enough. That's where I am trying to live."

I have staked my claim in Psalm 91, and I have made this psalm a personal claim where all of my irons are fired. The results I have seen are too great to explain, and I *know* that my God is more than enough.

When Moses staked his claim, he really saw results! He was saying, "My God is more than enough to feed two million people. My God is all-sufficient. And even though we're in the wilderness, these two million people will have water. No matter how tough the circumstances may appear, I'm counting on El Shaddai to bring us through!" And He always did bring them through. This is why Hebrews 11 tells us that Moses forsook the pleasures of living in Pharaoh's house to sojourn in the wilderness with the children of Israel by faith (see Heb. 11:23-28). Moses stretched out his faith and said, "I don't need the comforts of Pharaoh's house, for my Almighty God has all that I need!"

Throughout his walk with the Lord—Elohim, Jehovah, and El Shaddai—Moses continued to witness the miraculous hand of God overcome nature itself. For 40 years the Israelites had no lack of their needs of food, water, or clothing. Their shoes did not wear out (see Deut. 29:5)!

That is just tremendous. And think about it; if God could do it back then for two million people, don't you think He will take care of you now? Stake your claim under the shadow of El Shaddai. He's more than enough, more than we will ever need in our lives! Take advantage of what Moses knew. God put it into writing for your use, so learn from Moses' knowledge and don't go through your life making stupid mistakes.

Do You Know El Shaddai's Provision Firsthand?

Do you want to dwell in the secret place of the most high God? Do you want to abide under the shadow of the Almighty?

I will say of the Lord, He is my refuge and my fortress: my God; in Him will I trust (Psalm 91:2).

Stake your claim with your mouth. Moses did just that, and you should too. Begin saying what you need God to be in your situation: "He's more than enough to heal me; He's more than enough to meet my financial needs; He's more than enough to the people that I teach to repent; He's more than enough to put new hearts in my children; He's more than enough to secure my job; He's more than enough to keep the love of Jesus Christ in my family; He's more than enough to open blind eyes; He's more than enough to keep me in perfect peace; and He's more than enough to keep me searching His Word and seeking His ways for my life."

Live under the shadow of the knowledge of a God who is more than enough. He will turn natural things around to make sure you will come through completely whole and completely blessed!

Holiness and Obedience Protect the Claim God Has Given You

Have you ever heard of "claim jumpers"? In the history of our midwestern states there were people who would stake a claim on land that already belonged to someone else. Sometimes they even removed another person's claim markers and put theirs up instead. These people were called "claim jumpers."

Well, the devil is a claim jumper, and he's trying to steal what you have claimed. But the Bible says He who promised is faithful and unmovable (see Heb. 10:23; 12:28). When the devil comes to steal your claim, you have to push the devil right back off your claim! The devil is mighty in deception. He will even try to "borrow" your claim, but don't let him have *any* room in your life.

You may have already moved off of your claim, it may have been by telling a little untruth, by cheating on your timecard at work, by eating one cookie in the supermarket, or even by eating one or two grapes at the store—just to test them before you bought them. These "little" things open the door to your darkness and to the god of darkness to reign over you. If this describes your condition, repent and get back in the swing of life. Confess with your mouth unto righteousness. When you do, He will not only forgive you, but He will also cleanse you of all unrighteousness (see 1 Jn. 1:9). Put yourself back into the hands of the all-sufficient One.

El Shaddai tells us that we can do nothing without Him (see Jn. 15:5). The Gospel of John tells us that we *must* be connected to Jesus, the all-sufficient Vine—El Shaddai and Elohim.

> *I am the true vine, and My Father is the husbandman. Every branch in Me that beareth not fruit He taketh away: and every branch that beareth fruit, He purgeth it, that it may bring forth more fruit. Now ye are clean through the word which I have spoken unto you. Abide in Me, and I in you. As the branch cannot bear fruit of itself, except it abide in the vine; no more can ye, except ye abide in Me. I am the vine, ye are the branches: He that abideth in Me, and I in him, the same bringeth forth much fruit: for without Me you can do nothing. If a man abide not in Me, he is cast forth as a branch, and is withered* [separated from God]*; and men* [the devil] *gather them, and cast them into the fire, and they are burned* [destroyed by the devil]*. If ye abide in Me, and My words abide in you, ye shall ask what ye will, and it shall be done unto you. Herein is My Father* [Elohim] *glorified, that ye bear much fruit; so shall ye be My disciples* [be like Jesus] (John 15:1-8).

You cannot stand in the middle and choose neither—it's either blessing and abundance or wrath. The day is coming when God will judge the earth. Choose His abundance. Choose for Him to be all-sufficient in every one of your situations. El Shaddai wants you to camp under Him! Repent and stake your claim for His abundance.

Chapter 4

Adonai

The names we have seen thus far—Elohim, Jehovah, and El Shaddai—relate to facets that display the person of God. *Elohim* expresses God as a God of might and power! *Jehovah* expresses God in His holiness and righteousness, the God-Redeemer. And His personality is expressed thus far by *El Shaddai*, a wonderful God of blessing and all-sufficiency.

Now we will look at God as *Adonai*. It is translated in the King James Bible Version of the Bible as *Lord*. This name reflects control and ownership, for we are owned by God. It also states our responsibility to God as His servants.

Our Lord Desires for Us to Know Him

Our Lord wants us to know just how special we are to Him. *Adonai* will help us to get to know Him with such truth that we will not only desire a deep relationship with Him but we will also be able to make a commitment to Him out of love and not fear. Adonai wants you to be as excited about Him as He is about you.

Adonai is used over 300 times in the Old Testament alone, and it literally means "Master"; "Owner"; or "Lord." There is an interesting characteristic of the name *Adonai* that it shares with the name *Elohim*. *Adonai* can be translated as being both *plural* and *possessive*. Therefore it confirms the tri-union of the Godhead: Father, Son, and Holy Spirit.

When describing men, the single word *adon* is used. However, when describing God, the word receives a suffix that makes it plural—*Adonai*. How exciting it is to see God the Father, Jesus, and the Holy Spirit all involved in this wonderful name. One of the psalmists says the following about Adonai:

The Lord said unto my Lord, Sit Thou at My right hand, until I make Thine enemies Thy footstool (Psalm 110:1).

The New Testament confirms Psalm 110:

Therefore let all the house of Israel know assuredly, that God hath made that same Jesus, whom ye have crucified, both Lord and Christ (Acts 2:36).

God, our Adonai, is our master. The Gospel of John tells us of how Simon Peter accepted Jesus as master.

Ye call Me Master and Lord: and ye say well; for so I am [the Lordship of Jesus refers back to the plural personality of the Godhead—Lord Elohim and Master Adonai]. *If I then, your Lord and Master, have washed your feet; ye also ought to wash one another's feet* (John 13:13-14).

God is our master, for we, this earth, have been purchased back with the price of God's own blood. We are His purchased possession.

A Bondslave Serves Out of Love

Exodus 21 gives us a beautiful picture of this relationship.

Now these are the judgments which thou shalt set before them. If thou buy an Hebrew servant, six years he shall serve: and in the seventh he shall go out free for nothing. If he came in by himself, he shall go out by himself: if he were married, then his wife shall go out with him. If his master have given him a wife, and she have born him sons or daughters; the wife and her children shall be her master's, and he shall go out by himself. And if the servant shall plainly say, I love my master, my wife, and my children; I will not go out free: then his master shall bring him unto the judges; he shall also bring him to the door, or unto the door post; and his master shall bore his ear through with an awl; and he shall serve him for ever (Exodus 21:1-6).

The Israelites permitted limited slavery. If a man was poverty stricken and unable to meet financial needs, he could say to another Israelite who had wealth, "Could I be your slave for six years?" As a slave, this man would be responsible to obey every order given him, and his master would be unto him all that he needed. Slaves were subject to all their master's desires.

After serving his master for six years, a slave was allowed to go free in the seventh year. At the time of his departure, a master was responsible to supply his former slave with a certain amount of material wealth. If a man was married before his enslavement and brought his wife with him, and if they had children, they all would go free. However, if the master had provided a wife for him, and if the wife had children, the wife and children would stay behind while the man left free. Naturally, a man who loves his wife and children will not go off and leave them behind. Therefore, he had the option to say to the master, "I will stay, for I love my master, my wife, and my children."

If the man was a good servant and the master desired to keep him, the master would take the former servant to the judge. The judge would draw up papers to this keeping. At this time, the master would also pierce the servant's ear with an awl and place within the hole a symbol of his household and his ownership of the slave. What did this symbolize? This was the slave's way of saying "I am a slave of mine own free will. I will never be free; I am a slave to my master for life. I am my master's bondslave." God wants us to choose to serve Him wholly, and total commitment to Adonai means allowing Him to call the shots in our lives.

Adonai is the God who totally owns His people. He protects them, provides for them, and directs them. The servants of Adonai are those whom He chooses to serve Him because they love Him. We are His bondslaves.

Jesus, Our Example of Servanthood

The relationship of the bondslave to the master is also a beautiful illustration of the Father-Son relationship between God and Jesus. Jesus came to earth to redeem us out of obedience to the Father's will. He did not sin because He was here to carry out a responsibility His Father had given Him.

The Bible tells us that as Jesus' physical death approached, He entered into a garden called Gethsemane to pray:

...Father, if Thou be willing, remove this cup from Me: nevertheless not My will, but Thine, be done. And there appeared an angel unto Him from heaven, strengthening Him. And being in an agony He prayed more earnestly: and His sweat was as it were great drops of blood falling down to the ground (Luke 22:42-44).

Jesus faced a great struggle in the garden of Gethsemane that day. I also believe the Father said to Him, "Son, You don't have to drink of this cup, but it's for Your bride [Israel] and the children of Abraham, Isaac, and Jacob, as many as the sands of the shore [the Church]." By saying, "Not my will, but Yours be done," Jesus was saying, "I am more than My Father's servant; I am a bondslave to His will. I came here to complete His will, so I am willing to be pierced."

Adonai—Master and Lord of lords—is displayed through the Father, the Son, and the Holy Spirit. This is the promise of God being fulfilled as it was ordained in Genesis 3.

And the Lord God said unto the serpent, Because thou hast done this, thou art cursed above all cattle, and above every beast of the field; upon thy belly shalt thou go, and dust shalt thou eat all the days of thy life: and I will put enmity between thee and the woman, and between thy seed and her seed; it shall bruise thy head, and thou shalt bruise his heel (Genesis 3:14-15).

Jesus' hands and feet were nailed into the cross. His flesh was cruelly beaten, and He was pierced with a sword. Why? Because He became a bondslave to the Father, One who said, "No matter the cost, it's Your will, not Mine."

Jesus gave Himself with the attitude of a bondslave:

Let this mind be in you, which was also in Christ Jesus: who, being in the form of God, thought it not robbery to be equal with God: but made Himself of no reputation, and took upon Him the form of a servant, and was made in the likeness of men (Philippians 2:5-7).

Jesus, the bondslave to His Father, willingly hung upon the tree. He was willingly pierced because of His love for us. Today, He still carries the signs of His bondslavery and sacrifice. Old Testament slaves had their ears pierced. Jesus' enslavement took Him far past that: He has scars upon His hands, His feet, His head, His back, and His side. These marks all say one thing: *bondslave.*

Zechariah 12:10 tells us, "...they shall look upon Me whom they have pierced, and they shall mourn for Him, as one mourneth for his only son...." The people who pierced Jesus will look upon Him again in the day of judgment.

Psalm 110:1; Acts 2:36; and Zechariah 12:10 all confirm the plurality within the name Adonai.

Freedom From Full Submission to Our Master

Some people cringe at the thought of God having complete ownership over them. People who have been conformed to the world's image and perspective say, "I have to be my own person," or "I'm just a free spirit." Hogwash! You are not a free spirit! You have been purchased by the Lord at the most expensive price—His own blood.

Till we all come in the unity of the faith, and of the knowledge of the Son of God, unto a perfect man [perfection], unto the measure of the stature of the fulness of Christ: that we henceforth be no more children, tossed to and fro, and carried about with every wind of doctrine, by the sleight of men, and cunning craftiness, whereby they lie in wait to deceive (Ephesians 4:13-14).

The only free spirit is the Holy Spirit. Whosoever is in agreement with the Father and the Son, it is he who becomes a bondslave to Adonai, and it is he who will be free in Him.

The nature of man is evil—since the fall of Adam. The Bible tells us this about our nature:

But even unto this day, when Moses is read, the veil is upon their heart. Nevertheless when it shall turn to the

Lord, the veil shall be taken away. Now the Lord is that Spirit: and where the Spirit of the Lord is, there is liberty. But we all, with open face beholding as in a glass the glory of the Lord, are changed into the same image from glory to glory, even as by the Spirit of the Lord (2 Corinthians 3:15-18).

Adonai Calls People to His Service

Adonai, Master! Isaiah was willing to be a bondslave for God. He wrote the Book of Isaiah. He ministered to four kings, and he had the greatest revelation of the Son of God than was received by any of the other prophets. He saw the redemption of Jesus Christ. This is why his book is called "The Gospel of the Old Testament."

When Isaiah saw the Lord as his master and owner, he reacted by saying, "I am a man of unclean lips." When he said that, a seraphim placed a white-hot coal upon his lip, and the Lord began to speak to him about his responsibility.

In the year that King Uzziah died I saw also the Lord sitting upon a throne, high and lifted up, and His train filled the temple. ... Then said I, Woe is me! for I am undone; because I am a man of unclean lips, and I dwell in the midst of a people of unclean lips: for mine eyes have seen the King, the Lord of hosts. Then flew one of the seraphims unto me, having a live coal in his hand, which he had taken with the tongs from off the altar: and he laid it upon my mouth, and said, Lo, this hath touched thy lips; and thine iniquity is taken away, and thy sin purged. Also I heard the voice of the Lord, saying, Whom shall I send, and who will go for Us? Then said I, Here am I; send me (Isaiah 6:1,5-8).

The Book of Acts, chapter 9, tells us of a young man who called God *Adonai*. He was on the road to Damascus, on his way to persecute and kill the Christians. As he travelled, suddenly a brilliant light shone upon him, blinding his eyes. Then a voice spoke, "Saul, Saul, why persecutest thou Me?" Quickly Saul's heart was softened and the Lord could deal with him. This is evidenced by Saul's words, "You are my Lord and Master!" (See Acts 9:1-8.)

If we acknowledge God as Lord and Master, it will bring forth revelation knowledge of God and His Word (see Job 28:28). By calling to God as Adonai, Saul received wonderful revelation.

...And the Lord said, I am Jesus whom thou persecutest: it is hard for thee to kick against the pricks (Acts 9:5).

Saul saw Jesus as the Lord of his life and the master of all that he was. God changed Saul's name to Paul and continued to give him revelation knowledge. As time passed, Paul wrote almost one-third of the New Testament because at the beginning of his spiritual life he not only took Jesus as Savior, but he took Him also as Lord, Adonai! You too must take Him as your master.

Adonai Keeps Close to His Willing Servants

In Acts 23 Paul was in big trouble with the Jews. He was teaching, and the Jews were in hot disagreement with what he was teaching. So they started plans to kill him. Paul said, "It's not me...the real problem is that the Sadducees are mad with the Pharisees because the Pharisees believe in angels and the resurrection, and they are upset because I have been teaching *Adonai*, my Master and Lord!" (See Acts 23:6-9.)

God turned this situation around for Paul. He was about to be killed, but after he made that statement the Pharisees and the Sadducees began to fight among themselves. The night following this the Lord Himself came and encouraged His servant,

> *And the night following the Lord stood by him, and said, Be of good cheer, Paul: for as thou hast testified of Me in Jerusalem, so must thou bear witness also at Rome* (Acts 23:11).

Paul's heart must have really been encouraged! His Master and Owner stood by him. Paul called on the Lord because he needed protection that only his Master could give.

> *For he that is called in the Lord, being a servant* [bondslave], *is the Lord's freeman: likewise also he that is called, being free, is Christ's servant* (1 Corinthians 7:22).

A whole commitment is essential in order to have results! If you want to be totally free, be 100 percent committed to the Lord as His bondslave. When you place Him in command of your life and follow His direction, you are free from fear, worry, and anything that lurks in darkness! *You are free!!*

You can affect the direction of your nation by calling on God as your Adonai! Let Him be your Savior, and let Him be Lord to you, for you, and in you.

Jesus wants to be more than just your Savior. He wants to be your Adonai, your Master and Owner. The Scriptures offer us a beautiful picture of our relationship with Him:

The Security of the Godly

He that dwelleth in the secret place of the most High shall abide under the shadow of the Almighty. I will say of the Lord, He is my refuge and my fortress: my God; in Him will I trust. Surely He shall deliver thee from the snare of the fowler, and from the noisome pestilence. He shall cover thee with His feathers, and under His wings shalt thou trust: His truth shall be thy shield and buckler. Thou shalt not be afraid for the terror by night; nor for the arrow that flieth by day; nor for the pestilence that walketh in darkness; nor for the destruction that wasteth at noonday. A thousand shall fall at thy side, and ten thousand at thy right hand; but it shall not come nigh thee. Only with thine eyes shalt thou behold and see the reward of the wicked. Because thou hast made the Lord, which is my refuge, even the most High, thy habitation; there shall no evil befall thee, neither shall any plague come nigh thy dwelling. For He shall give His angels charge over thee, to keep thee in all thy ways. They shall bear thee up in their hands, lest thou dash thy foot against a stone. Thou shalt tread upon the lion and adder: the young lion and the dragon shalt thou trample under feet. Because he hath set his love upon Me, therefore will I deliver him: I will set him on high, because he hath known My name. He shall call upon Me, and I will answer him: I will be with him in trouble; I will deliver him, and honour him. With long life will I satisfy him, and shew him My salvation (Psalm 91:1-16).

Do you know Him as your personal Adonai?

Adonai Empowers His Servants to Rule in His Name

Adonai, our Lord and Master, is the One who releases all His provision for us when we let Him have full charge of our lives.

But as many as received Him, to them gave He power to become the sons of God, even to them that believe on His name: which were born, not of blood, nor of the will of the flesh, nor of the will of man, but of God (John 1:12-13).

When we receive Jesus, Adonai, He gives us the power to become sons of God. By becoming a son of God, you also become a brother of Adonai—Jesus, the Christ. You become a living branch of God!

John 15 teaches how we are then empowered by Elohim:

I am the true vine, and My Father is the husbandman. Every branch in Me that beareth not fruit He taketh away: and every branch that beareth fruit, He purgeth it, that it may bring forth more fruit (John 15:1-2).

Now a farmer or a gardener will not go and trim, purge, or dress another farmer's plants, unless he has permission or is a sharecropper. Otherwise, this would be an unlawful act and would cause great strife between the two gardeners. This illustrates why John 1:1-2 is such an important passage of Scripture as it relates to our relationship with Adonai.

Adonai is also our cleaner, for one must be clean before going before pure and mighty Elohim.

Now ye are clean through the word which I have spoken unto you. Abide in Me, and I in you. As the branch cannot bear fruit of itself, except it abide in the vine; no more can ye, except ye abide in Me. I am the vine, ye are the branches: He [Elohim] that abideth in Me, and I in him, the same bringeth forth much fruit: for without Me [Adonai] ye can do nothing. If a man abide not in me, he is cast forth as a branch, and is withered; and men gather them, and cast them into the fire, and they are burned. If ye abide in Me, and My words abide in you, ye shall ask what ye will, and it shall be done unto you. Herein is My Father glorified, that ye bear much fruit; so shall ye be My disciples (John 15:3-8).

The next few verses of the chapter explain the father-son relationship we have with God as we abide in Christ.

As the Father hath loved Me, so have I loved you: continue ye in My love. If ye keep My commandments, ye shall abide in My love; even as I have kept My Father's commandments, and abide in His love. These things have I spoken unto you, that My joy might remain in you, and that your joy might be full. This is My commandment, That ye love one another, as I have loved you. Greater love hath no man than this, that a man lay down his life for his friends. Ye are My friends, if ye do whatsoever I command you. Henceforth, I call you not servants; for the servant knoweth not what his lord doeth: but I have called you friends; for all things that I have heard of My Father I have made known unto you. Ye have not chosen Me, but I have chosen you, and ordained you, that ye should go and bring forth fruit, and that your fruit should remain: that whatsoever ye shall ask of the Father in My name, He may give it you. These things I command you, that ye love one another (John 15:9-17).

The relationship we have with Elohim (through Adonai) gives us the power to become adonais, masters and owners! As Jesus has said, we are no more servants, but friends. And friends receive all the things that the Father has given Him because Christ has given them to us.

Then the same day at evening, being the first day of the week, when the doors were shut where the disciples were assembled for fear of the Jews, came Jesus and stood in the midst, and saith unto them, Peace be unto you. And when He had so said, He shewed unto them His hands and His side. Then were the disciples glad, when they saw the Lord. Then said Jesus to them again, Peace be unto you: as My Father hath sent Me,

*even so send I you. And when He had said this, He
breathed on them, and saith unto them, Receive ye the
Holy Ghost: whosesoever sins ye remit, they are remit-
ted unto them; and whosesoever sins ye retain, they are
retained* (John 20:19-23).

These Scriptures are given by Adonai, and clearly
they tell man that as Jesus was a man on earth, so are we
expected to be the same as Jesus was then! For now
Jesus is not only Adonai, but also El Shaddai and Elohim! He is a God that is more than enough, and He
wants all of His people to be as He made them to be.

Here are some other Scriptures that tell us what is
expected of man in Jesus:

*Neither pray I for these alone, but for them also which
shall believe on Me through their word; that they all
may be one; as Thou, Father, art in Me, and I in Thee,
that they also may be one in Us: that the world may believe that Thou hast sent Me. And the glory which
Thou gavest Me I have given them; that they may be
one, even as We are one: I in them, and Thou in Me,
that they may be made perfect in one; and that the
world may know that Thou hast sent Me, and hast
loved them, as Thou hast loved Me. Father, I will that
they also, whom Thou hast given Me, be with Me where
I am; that they may behold My glory, which Thou hast
given Me: for Thou lovedst Me before the foundation of
the world. O righteous Father, the world hath not
known Thee: but I have known Thee, and these have
known that Thou hast sent Me. And I have declared*

unto them Thy name, and will declare it: that the love wherewith Thou hast loved Me may be in them, and I in them (John 17:20-26).

In Jesus, Our Adonai

In Him, we are promised the Spirit.

If ye love Me, keep My commandments. And I will pray the Father, and He shall give you another Comforter, that He may abide with you for ever; even the Spirit of truth; whom the world cannot receive, because it seeth Him not, neither knoweth Him: but ye know Him; for He dwelleth with you, and shall be in you. I will not leave you comfortless: I will come to you. Yet a little while, and the world seeth me no more; but ye see Me: because I live, ye shall live also. At that day ye shall know that I am in My Father, and ye in Me, and I in you. He that hath My commandments, and keepeth them, he it is that loveth Me: and he that loveth Me shall be loved of My Father, and I will love him, and will manifest Myself to him. Judas saith unto him, not Iscariot, Lord, how is it that Thou wilt manifest Thyself unto us, and not unto the world? Jesus [Adonai] answered and said unto him, If a man love Me, he will keep My words: and My Father will love him, and We will come unto him, and make Our abode with him. He that loveth Me not keepeth not My sayings: and the word which ye hear is not Mine, but the Father's which sent me (John 14:15-24).

He also promises us peace.

These things have I spoken unto you, being yet present with you. But the Comforter, which is the Holy Ghost, whom the Father will send in My name, He shall teach you all things, and bring all things to your remembrance, whatsoever I have said unto you. Peace I leave with you, My peace I give unto you: not as the world giveth, give I unto you. Let not your heart be troubled, neither let it be afraid (John 14:25-27).

The Power of Confessing Our Faith

Seeing then that we have a great high priest, that is passed into the heavens, Jesus [Adonai] *the Son of God, let us hold fast our profession* (Hebrews 4:14).

The Greek word used for *profession* can also be rendered "confession." One thing too few of us realize is that our confessions rule us. Whenever we use the word *confession* people instinctively think of confessing sin, and the Bible does say, "If we confess our sins, He is faithful and just to forgive us our sins and to cleanse us from all unrighteousness" (1 Jn. 1:9). But that is the negative side of confession. The Bible has much more to say about the positive side of confessing our faith.

That if thou shalt confess with thy mouth the Lord Jesus, and shalt believe in thine heart that God hath raised Him from the dead, thou shalt be saved. For with the heart man believeth unto righteousness; and with the mouth confession is made unto salvation (Romans 10:9-10).

Thou art snared with the words of thy mouth, thou art taken with the words of thy mouth (Proverbs 6:2).

Jesus said what we say is our confession, and the words we confess rule us! God saw that His people were dying daily because of the lack of knowledge (see Hos. 4:6a), and He wanted so much for man to live that He prepared for man a guide book. If man will follow His guidelines, He will live and return to life.

Speaking of confession, Proverbs 18:20 tells us, "A man's belly shall be satisfied with the fruit [word] of his mouth [confession]; and with the increase of his lips shall he be filled." To clarify this Scripture, the fruit of man's mouth is the words he speaks. The speaking is his confession, and the increase of his speaking is what he will be filled with. Therefore if your words are bad words, that is what your life will be. And if your words are good words, your life will be good. By your words you may have life in your environment or death in your environment. Consider the following verse.

Death and life are in the power of the tongue: and they that love it shall eat the fruit thereof (Proverbs 18:21).

(Note: the word *fruit* is singular, so Proverbs 18:21 is saying you will produce one fruit or the other—good or bad, not good and bad.)

In Adonai, your words are power. The same power Jesus spake with is the same power you speak with. What the writer in Proverbs is saying is that man only speaks out of the fruit he has within him, either death or life.

Do Not Doubt the Power of Your Words

For verily I say unto you, That whosoever shall say unto this mountain, Be thou removed, and be thou cast into the sea; and shall not doubt in his heart, but shall believe that those things which he saith shall come to pass; he shall have whatsoever he saith (Mark 11:23).

Let's meditate on these words of Jesus a little more, "...whosoever shall say...and shall not doubt in his heart, but shall believe that those things which he saith shall come to pass; he shall have whatsoever he saith." Did Jesus know what He was talking about? Are these merely the words of someone who was dreaming or being irresponsible? No! These are not words of a dreamer! Jesus meant exactly what He said. Now, what did He say you shall have? He said you shall have what you say. If you really believe a thing in your heart, positive or negative, and you say it with your mouth, you will really have it. Jesus said you would.

It's always with the heart that man believes and with the mouth that confession is made unto any of the provisions of God. Notice how these two verses of God's Word say the same thing in different words.

For with the heart man believeth unto righteousness; and with the mouth confession is made unto salvation (Romans 10:10).

And the Lord said, If ye had faith as a grain of mustard seed, ye might say unto this sycamine tree, Be thou plucked up by the root, and be thou planted in the sea; and it should obey you (Luke 17:6).

And Jesus said unto them...If ye have faith as a grain of mustard seed, ye shall say unto this mountain, Remove hence to yonder place; and it shall remove; and nothing shall be impossible unto you (Matthew 17:20).

Jesus answered and said unto them, Verily I say unto you, If ye have faith, and doubt not, ye shall not only do this which is done to the fig tree, but also if ye shall say unto this mountain, Be thou removed, and be thou cast into the sea; it shall be done. And all things, whatsoever ye shall ask in prayer, believing, ye shall receive (Matthew 21:21-22).

Hebrews 4:14 tells us to "Hold fast our profession." We have already noted that modern translators render it, "Let us hold fast our *confession*." What is the confession we are to hold fast to? What is the confession we are to maintain? It is the confession of our faith in the Lord Jesus Christ; the confession of our faith in God our Heavenly Father; the confession of our faith in the Word of God.

The majority of Christians, although sincere, are very weak. This is because they never really confess what God's Word says about them. They don't dare confess that they are what the Bible says they are and that they have what the Bible says they have.

Truthfully, many maintain a wrong confession instead of holding fast to a right confession. A wrong confession is a confession of defeat, of failure, and of the supremacy of satan. These people are always talking about what a time they're having with the devil—what a battle they're having with all they are going through, how the devil is keeping them from success and from health, and how the devil has them in such bondage. According to what Jesus said, what you say is what you get. The bellys of these people will be full of the fruit of their lips.

In my heart I believe that people wouldn't speak this way if they really knew what they were doing, because that kind of confession is an unconscious declaration that God, our heavenly Father, is a failure. God is not a failure! He simply cannot fail. Defeat is not in God, nor is there any defeat *of* God! When you talk about defeat you're talking about the works of the devil. God did not intend that you (a part of His Church) should be defeated. He said that the gates of hell would not prevail against you (the Church)! (See Matthew 16:18.)

Testimony is part of life. If you want to develop a robust life, then be a continuous confessor of what God is doing in your life. Be a Job! Job gave God credit for all things. So practice a good confession. The more you talk about the things of God, the more real He will become to you. Therefore, when you speak, speak godly. Life is like love, it is of the heart and the spirit. Like love, it lives and finds its joy in its continual confession.

Jesus Confessed His Calling

If you carefully examine the life of Jesus you'll find that, from the beginning of His public ministry until He was led to the cross, Jesus forever confessed who He is, what He is, and what His mission was! For example, He said, "I came forth from the Father, and am come into the world: again, I leave the world, and go to the Father" (Jn. 16:28). This was a four-part confession; it covered His life from Incarnation to Ascension.

One of the most powerful confessions Jesus made was, "He that hath seen Me hath seen the Father..." (Jn. 14:9b). What a bold confession: "If you want to see the Father, look on Me." In John 12, it is recorded that He said, "...he that seeth Me seeth Him that sent Me. I am come a light into the world, that whosoever believeth on Me should not abide in darkness" (Jn. 12:45-46).

It can't be expressed too much, so let's say it again: Jesus constantly confessed who He is, what He is, and what His mission was in life. All of us say, "But He was Jesus...." Yes, I know. But the Bible teaches that Jesus left us an example and that we should follow in His steps. In John 13 Jesus says, "For I have given you an example, that ye should do as I have done to you" (Jn. 13:15).

Jesus held fast His confession, so let us hold our confession. The Bible tells us that Jesus is Adonai. The Bible also tells us that we, as flesh, are sons of God. When we receive Jesus as our Redeemer, He gives us power to become sons of God (see Jn. 1:12).

Adonai Wants Us to Reflect His Image

Here are some Scriptures we can confess daily to help us become more like Jesus:

For ye have not received the spirit of bondage again to fear; but ye have received the Spirit of adoption, whereby we cry, Abba, Father. The Spirit itself beareth witness with our spirit, that we are the children of God: and if children, then heirs; heirs of God, and joint-heirs with Christ; if so be that we suffer with Him, that we may be also glorified together (Romans 8:15-17).

But God, who is rich in mercy, for His great love where-with He loved us, even when we were dead in sins, hath quickened us together with Christ, (by grace ye [we] *are saved;) and hath raised us up together, and made us sit together in heavenly places in Christ Jesus: that in the ages to come He might shew the exceeding riches of His grace in His kindness toward us through Christ Jesus* (Ephesians 2:4-7).

But now in Christ Jesus ye who sometimes were far off are made nigh by the blood of Christ. For He is our peace, who hath made both one, and hath broken down the middle wall of partition between us; having abolished in His flesh the enmity, even the law of commandments contained in ordinances; for to make in Himself of twain one new man, so making peace; and that He might reconcile both unto God in one body by the cross, having slain the enmity thereby: and came and preached peace to you which were afar off, and to them that were nigh. For through Him we both have access by one Spirit unto the Father. Now therefore ye [we] *are no more strangers and foreigners, but fellow-citizens with the saints, and of the household of God* (Ephesians 2:13-19).

Salutations
and Thanksgiving

David, an apostle of Jesus Christ by the will of God, to the saints and faithful brethren in Christ Jesus: Grace be unto you, and peace, from God our Father and the Lord Jesus Christ. I give thanks to God the Father of my Lord Jesus Christ, for through His love for me, He has made it possible for the life of Christ to be in me. I also thank God for His longsuffering patience with me, the same patience He exhibited toward Noah, Abraham, Isaac, Jacob, Moses, and many others. By His patience I have been brought to this point in my life at which I can receive my instruction from Him, words that bear witness with His written Word and teach me His way as I have asked Him. I also give thanks to God for His love that never leaves us. He is the Father of the sinners, and through Him we are made righteous. I give thanks to the Holy Spirit for bearing witness with my spirit, inspiring me to write as I have. God I bless you in the name of Jesus. Amen.

Doxology:
That's My King!

The Bible says…

My King is a seven-way king. He's King of the Jews—
that's a radical king. He's King of Israel—that's a na-
tional king. He's King of righteousness. He's King of
the ages. He's King of Heaven. He's King of glory. He's
a King of kings, and He's the Lord of lords. That's my
King!

Well, I wonder do you know Him? David did, for he
stated, "The heavens declare the glory of God; and the
firmament sheweth His handiwork" (Ps. 19:1). My King
is a sovereign king. No means of measure can define
His limitless love; no far-seeing telescope can bring into
view any boundary to his endless supply; no barrier can
hinder Him from bestowing His blessings. He's endur-
ingly strong. He's entirely sincere. He's eternally stead-
fast. He's infinitely graceful. He's imperially powerful.
He's impartially merciful.

Do You Know Him?

He's the greatest phenomenon ever to cross the horizon of this world—He's God's Son. He's the sinner's Savior. He's the centerpiece of civilization. He stands in the solitude of Himself. He's august and unique, unparalleled and unprecedented. He is the loftiest idea in literature. He's the highest personality in philosophy. He is the supreme problem in higher criticism. He is the fundamental doctrine of true theology. He is the core, the necessity for true, spiritual religion. He is the miracle of the ages. He is the superlative of everything good that you choose to call Him. He's the only One qualified to be your all-sufficient Savior!

Do You Know Him Today?

He supplies strength to the weak. He aids the tempted and the tried. He sympathizes and He saves. He strengthens and sustains. He guards and He guides. He heals the sick. He cleanses the lepers. He forgives sinners and discharges debtors. He delivers the captives. He defends the feeble. He blesses the young. He regards the aged. He serves the unfortunate. He rewards the diligent, and He purifies the meek.

I Wonder Do You Know Him?

My King is a key to knowledge. He is a wellspring of wisdom. He is a doorway of deliverance. He's a pathway of peace. He is a roadway of righteousness. He's a highway of holiness. He's a gateway of glory.

His office is manifold. His promise is sure. His light is matchless. His goodness is limitless. His mercy is everlasting. His love never changes. His Word is enough, and His grace is sufficient. His reign is one of righteousness. His yoke is easy, and His burden is light (see Mt. 11:30).

I wish I could describe Him to you, but He's indescribable! He's incomprehensible. He's invincible. He's irresistible. You can't get Him out of your mind. You can't outlive Him, and you can't live without Him. The Pharisees couldn't stand Him, but they found out they couldn't stop Him. Pilate couldn't find any fault in Him (see Lk. 23:4). The witnesses couldn't get their testimonies to agree. Herod couldn't kill Him. Death couldn't handle Him and the grave couldn't hold Him!

Yes, That's my King! That's my King! That's my King!!

For His is the Kingdom and the power and the glory forever and ever and ever and ever.... When you get through with all of the forevers, then amen, amen, amen!